AF885590

YOUR GUIDE TO ROAD CYCLING SAFETY IN COLORADO

10 Critical Steps Colorado Bicyclists Should Take To Protect Themselves On Our Roadways

INFORMATION THAT MAY HELP SAVE YOUR LIFE AND GUIDE YOU THROUGH THE ROADBLOCKS OF RESOLVING YOUR BICYCLE ACCIDENT CLAIM

Bryan S. VanMeveren, Esq.

ISBN: 978-1-941645-89-5

Designed and Published by:
Speakeasy Publications
73-03 Bell Blvd, #10
Oakland Gardens, NY 11364
www.SpeakeasyMarketingInc.com
(888) 225-8594

Disclaimer

This publication is intended to be informational only. No legal advice is being given, and no attorney-client relationship is intended to be created by reading this material. If you are facing legal issues, whether criminal or civil, seek professional legal counsel to get your questions answered.

VANMEVEREN LAW GROUP, P.C.
2038 Caribou Drive, Suite 101
Fort Collins, CO 80525
(970) 495-9741
www.vanmeverenlaw.com

TESTIMONIALS

"Our thank you is long overdue but... It is with sincere deep gratitude that we accept all that you have so graciously done for us. The list is long. The meal, the behind the scenes organization of all the fifth grade families wanting to help and the legal help is also appreciated. It has become very apparent to us the burden you have lifted off of our shoulders every time we get a copy of the correspondence you have sent out on our behalf. We are truly astounded by your generosity. It's hard to be on the receiving end of so much generosity. You make it doable, albeit still very humbling. Please continue to keep us in your prayers. Your prayers are most important to us and give us great comfort."

- R. and P.

"I want to take this moment to thank you personally for the effort and compassion you put forth in achieving the best possible outcome for my family and me. The months since my husband's death have not been easy. Your success in my case has made the months more bearable. Thank you for giving me great direction. May God bless you, your family and your staff. God blessed me when you became a part of my life. Thank you again for your kindness and continued friendship."

- J.W.

"VanMeveren Law Group, P.C., is personable and professional and serves the clients extremely well. I could not have been happier with their expertise and service."

- Personal Injury Client

"Bryan is extremely knowledgeable and personable with clients. He is a great advocate and makes every effort to assure that the needs of his clients are met. He anticipates problems before they become issues and goes above and beyond to meet his clients' needs. He is a good communicator and keeps clients abreast of the process and potential outcomes. As a client, I felt very confident with Bryan; he is very honest, fair and straightforward."

- Personal Injury Client

"Thank you for all your help with the medical and vehicle settlements. We appreciate all you have done for our family. Please accept this gift certificate for dinner as a gesture of our gratitude. We would also like to give this donation to the Boys & Girls Clubs of Larimer County in your name. We have been blessed to have your help through this tough time. Thank you. May God bless you and your family."

- G., C., M. and S.

"Bryan and his associates showed empathy and compassion in the way his staff treated me personally as well as in how my case was handled. His honesty, patience and dedication to the law showed in his emails and conversations. I was informed on a constant basis and never felt left out of even the smallest decisions. When all was said and done, and the outcome of my particular case was presented, I felt justice was served."

- Personal Injury Client

"Bryan has represented my wife and me for two injury accident claims. His expertise, professionalism and legal counsel is second to none. In both situations, we were very satisfied with the results and outcome of our claims and felt we were represented in the best professional manner possible. My wife and I strongly recommend Bryan VanMeveren."

- Personal Injury Client

"Bryan VanMeveren defended me in a personal injury case. I would highly recommend Bryan for his knowledge and his assertiveness in arguing these types of cases. Bryan has always been very responsive to requests and was very patient in letting me take my time in settling the case."

- Personal Injury Client

"Thank you again for agreeing to take my case. I am very grateful for all you did. I realize how complicated my case ended up being, and how fortunate I was to have you represent me. And I appreciate the discount you gave. The settlement you negotiated was far more than I had hoped for!"

- M.

TABLE OF CONTENTS

AUTHOR INTRODUCTION

Bryan S. VanMeveren is admitted to practice in the State and Federal Courts of Colorado, Wyoming and Arizona. A former insurance defense litigator specializing in personal injury and bad faith cases, he uses his experience and expertise to obtain just results for victims of negligence. He obtained his undergraduate degree from the University of Wyoming and his Juris Doctorate from the University of South Dakota. He served for two years on the Colorado Supreme Court's standing committee on the Rules of Professional Conduct. He recently completed a six year term on the Eighth Judicial Nominating Commission, which is responsible for the selection of Larimer County District Court Judges.

For the past sixteen years, Mr. VanMeveren has volunteered his time with both Larimer County Pro Bono Intake Services and he serves as a speaker and legal aid for the county's Domestic Relations Program. He also serves as a representative on the county's Bench-Bar Committee, aimed at improving professionalism and ethics between attorneys and judges.

When not busy with his law practice, Mr. VanMeveren enjoys spending time with his wife of 27 years and his six children. He also enjoys working in his community. He worked as a volunteer board member and chief legal counsel for the Boys and Girls Clubs of Larimer County for five years and continues to serve as legal counsel and as an honorary board member. He also volunteers his time at running events benefitting local charities and coaches basketball at high school and recreational levels.

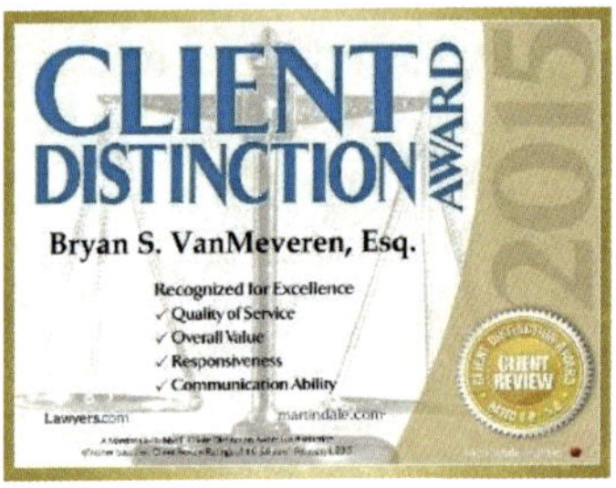

Mr. VanMeveren is an avid trail runner, cyclist, skier, triathlete and supporter of local health and fitness events. He ran the Boston Marathon and was a primary sponsor and served for twelve years as legal counsel for the Colorado Marathon, the largest marathon in northern Colorado. He remains very active in the local health and fitness community, volunteering his time and providing legal counsel to local race directors and health clubs.

VanMeveren Law Group also continues to sponsor numerous local charity runs and triathlons.

Mr. VanMeveren has completed over 25 marathons, 16 Ironman Triathlons, numerous Ultra Marathons, Xterra races, adventure races and bicycle races. He is a five-time Ironman World Championship Qualifier, a five-time Half Ironman World Championship Qualifier, an eight-time USA Triathlon All American and was named an Ironman All World Athlete in 2013, 2014 and 2015, with a #3 age group world ranking in 2015.

Areas of Practice

- Personal Injury-- Plaintiff
- Insurance Law
- Bicycle Accidents
- Insurance Bad Faith
- Motor Vehicle Accidents

Bar Admissions

- Colorado
- Wyoming
- Arizona
- U.S. Court of Appeals 9th Circuit
- U.S. Court of Appeals 10th Circuit

Education

- University of South Dakota School of Law, Vermillion, South Dakota
- Juris Doctorate
- University of Wyoming College of Health Sciences, Laramie, Wyoming
- Bachelor of Science

Honors and Awards

- Martindale Hubbell's AV Rating
- Lawyers.com Client Distinction Award

Pro Bono Activities

- Honorary Board Member, Boys and Girls Clubs of Larimer County
- Larimer County Pro Bono Intake
- Larimer County Domestic Relations Pro Bono Speaker
- Colorado Supreme Court Pro Bono Achievement Award

Publications

- ***Your Personal Injury Case***, Copyright 2015, Bryan S. VanMeveren

HOW COMMON ARE BICYCLE ACCIDENTS IN COLORADO?

Unfortunately, bicycle accidents in Colorado are becoming more and more common. Just this past year, Colorado's

population growth doubled national averages. That means more motorists on Colorado roads. Because Colorado is such a scenic place to ride, more cyclists are also on the roadways and more accidents are occurring. Unfortunately, our modern technology continues to create more distractions for motorists within their vehicles, particularly when it comes to cell phone calls and texting.

At VanMeveren Law Group, we make bike accident cases a priority. We've handled everything from the inattentive driver turning into the path of the cyclist, to numerous tragic "*dooring*" cases, to the truck driver who failed to follow the *three feet law* and sideswiped our cyclist client. We've helped the cyclist who was injured because of a dog owner who failed to restrain his pet, allowing it to run directly into our client's path. And we've assisted clients hurt by negligence due to poorly maintained sidewalks and improperly marked contstruction zones, all of which led to serious bike crashes. As fellow cyclists, we know how dangerous our roadways can be and we try to do everything we can to make our clients whole again and get them back to what they love to do: ride!

While it may be true that our community claims to be "biker friendly", inattentive driving remains a serious issue. Heavy vehicle traffic, combined with many roads that are not well designed for shared use with bicyclists, results in significant motorist/bicyclist interaction. Unfortunately, tragic collisions associated with inattentive driving and motorist/biker conflict have become all too common. According to the NHTSA Fatality Analysis Reporting System data, Colorado ranks as the 14th deadliest state to ride a bicycle with an average annual death toll of 10.

Bicyclists and motorists have many of the same rights and responsibilities, but bicyclists are the most vulnerable users of our Colorado roadways. Motorists need to understand that many situations occur when there is not a safe shoulder or a safe bike lane as they approach a cyclist from behind. In these instances, motorist patience and attentiveness are vital. One little distraction within a vehicle or an attempt to pass on a narrow stretch of roadway can instantly lead to the motorist hitting a bicyclist, causing devastating and life long harm.

Are Cyclists Required To Stay In The Bike Lane At All Times?

Bicyclists have every right to be in the through lane of

travel when conditions prevent them from safely traveling on the right side of the roadway or in the bike lane. Depending on the condition of the bike lane, sidewalk or road shoulder, the through lane may be the only safe and legal place for a cyclist to ride. Therefore, bicyclists are permitted to leave the bike lane for a variety of reasons. They may need to avoid being "*doored*" by a person getting out of a parked car. They may need to avoid hazards such as debris on the side of the road. They may be proceeding across a through lane to make a left hand turn. They may be positioning in a through lane to make themselves more visible and deter dangerous passing on narrow stretches of roadway. All of these maneuvers are legal and often necessary for cyclists to ride safely on our Colorado roads.

Are Helmets Required In Colorado?

Surprisingly, Colorado does not require that bicyclists wear helmets. Some local ordinances do require helmets, but not Colorado state law. Despite the lack of Colorado law governing the use of helmets, we hope that all cyclists will choose to play it safe and always wear a helmet when cycling.

What Is Colorado's "Dooring" Law?

A common issue that we've handled in numerous cases involves Colorado's "*dooring*" law. Colorado law, specifically C.R.S. 42-4-1207, requires that motorists open their car door on the side of moving traffic only after they've looked to make sure it is reasonably safe and can be done without interfering with traffic, including bicyclists. Failure to look before opening a car door can have dire consequences for an approaching cyclist. *Imagine a cyclist traveling at as little as 10 miles per hour and having a car door suddenly thrust open*

directly in his or her path. Sadly, we've seen these cases cause broken bones, head injuries and a tragic case where our client hit the car door, was thrown into through traffic and run over. Please look twice before opening your car door.

Can Cyclists Ride Two Abreast On The Roadway?

A common complaint of motorists in northern Colorado involves cyclists riding two abreast in the roadway. Understand that cyclists are permitted to ride two abreast, provided they are not

interfering with traffic, and they often do so to be more visible to motorists so as to discourage drivers from attempting to make a dangerous passing maneuver on a narrow road. Most cyclists will move to the side of the roadway when it is reasonably safe to do so, as to not interfere with the flow of traffic.

No doubt, motorists can certainly become frustrated with the slow pace of a cyclist when they're in a hurry to get somewhere. Please be cautious when driving your vehicle around or near cyclists. As the old Greek proverb says: *One minute of patience, ten years of peace.*

Do Road Hazards Often Lead To Bicycle Accidents?

The most common road hazards that bicyclists encounter are usually in the bike lane or on the shoulder of the road. Hazards can include anything from a pothole to a sewer grate,

a manhole cover, a construction cone, standing water, a parked car or an animal carcass. Bicyclists are also faced with construction debris, nails, sticks, posts and rebar. These cases involve crashes completely unrelated to motor vehicles, but can also result in very serious injuries. In some of these cases, there is liability or responsibility on the part of the city with regard to the condition of the roadway or with the company that dumped the materials on the roadway.

Road hazard claims are often aimed at the city for failing to properly maintain the road or leaving a large gap in a section of the road that causes the cyclist to crash. We have handled cases where bicyclist encountered construction debris and crashed. In those cases, it is vital to locate the construction company that dropped the materials and submit a claim to their insurance company. Unfortunately, in many of these cases, no responsible party can be located and the injured cyclist is left with lost earnings, pain and suffering, and no avenue of financial recovery for medical expenses.

Despite the many risks and hazards we face as Colorado cyclists, remember we are *not* above the law and should be held responsible when violating any of the same duties that apply to motorists. Thus, while bikers certainly have rights, they also have responsibilities including, but not limited to: following our traffic laws, not riding while under the influence of alcohol or drugs, yielding to pedestrians on sidewalks and dismounting when required in crosswalks.

See page 70, C.R.S. 42-4-1412, Operation of bicycles and other human-powered vehicles, for a legal description of our duties as Colorado cyclists.

10 Critical Steps Colorado Bicyclists Should Take To Protect Themselves On Our Roadways

1. Obey the rules of the road just as if you were operating a motor vehicle. Always follow the traffic laws, all traffic signals and any signs.

2. Wear your helmet and safety equipment: including glasses, reflective gear and gloves. Always carry a phone and identification. Use lights and reflectors, especially at night.

3. Unless you are avoiding hazards, passing another vehicle or preparing to make a left hand turn, try to ride with traffic and stay on the right side of the road and as far to the right as you can safely ride.

4. Try not to ride two abreast. While riding two abreast is legal in Colorado, it is much safer to ride single file. You do not want to impede the flow of traffic. Also, if you're riding single file, you're much less likely to irritate drivers and create unnecessary conflicts with motorists.

5. Always play it safe and ride in the lane of travel on narrow roads, hills and streets that do not have shoulders adequate for biking. *Take the lane* and ride with the flow of traffic. If you take the lane, be mindful of motorists approaching from behind. By taking the lane, the motorists will have to wait for a safe passing zone, rather than attempting to squeeze by, placing you in a dangerous situation.

6. Use the appropriate hand signals at all times to alert motorists of your intentions. Always signal your intentions as you approach an intersection.
7. Always try to make eye contact with the drivers at intersections.
8. Ride as straight as possible to make yourself more visible to motorists. Darting in and out of vehicle traffic is extremely dangerous.
9. *Never* assume that motorists are going to give you the right of way or that they even see you.
10. Ride in a manner that is defensive. Stay focused and be aware of your surroundings at all times.

What Types Of Injuries Do Bicycle Accident Victims Usually Experience?

The most common types of injuries that cyclists endure usually involve road rash, bruising, fractures and dislocations to the arms and legs. Shoulder separations, clavicle or collar bone fractures, wrist fractures and chest wall injuries are also quite common. Head injuries, including concussions, are also very common and that is why it is *critically important* that bicyclists wear helmets at all times, even though the law in Colorado does not require helmet use. Cases involving head injuries and traumatic brain injuries are numerous and the common sense way to protect yourself from a serious head injury is to wear a helmet. *According to the Insurance Institute for Highway Safety, use of a helmet has been estimated to reduce the risk of head injury by 85%.*

Does Your Bicycle Helmet Fit Properly?

Finding a good helmet is as easy as knowing these four tips.

1 SIZE

Try on several different helmets before you buy.

The best way to gauge comfort level and fit is through comparison. The helmet should fit comfortably all around your head. For a snug and secure fit, use additional pads.

2 STRAP

Pay attention to the chin strap and clasp.

Make sure that the chin strap fits around your ear and under your chin snugly and comfortably. The helmet should not shift or wobble on your head.

REMEMBER!

Once you've selected a helmet, wear it correctly every time you ride a bike.

3 STRAIGHT

Know how a helmet should fit.

A helmet is meant to be worn low on the forehead, just above your eyebrows. Look into a mirror or have a friend or parent help you determine the proper fit.

4 STICKER

Look for Snell certification.

Snell Memorial Foundation is a not-for-profit organization that independently tests helmets for safety. Snell standards are the most stringent in the world, exceeding those set by the ASTM & ANSI.

VLG IS IN YOUR CORNER

Our injury cases involving bicycle crashes have included spinal fractures, dislocations, punctured lungs, torn rotator cuffs, eye injuries, tibial plateau fractures, traumatic brain injuries, broken collar bones, severe road rash leading to scarring, fractured femurs and even death. Again, the most serious cases involve the head and the brain and most head injury cases involve extended recovery, extensive therapy, rehabilitation and permanent injuries. At VanMeveren Law Group, we make bicycle accident cases our top priority because, as fellow cyclists, we know how dangerous our Colorado roads are becoming and all cyclists need a strong advocate in their corner.

IMPORTANCE OF MEDICAL TREATMENT IN A BICYCLE ACCIDENT CLAIM

In order to effectively present your damages claim in a bicycle accident case, it is vital that you follow your medical providers' directives, make all scheduled medical appointments, document your out of pocket injury related expenses, keep a journal of your treatment and stay in consistent contact with your medical providers. If there is *any* question as to whether or not you are injured after a bicycle crash, immediately seek medical attention and get a proper evaluation. Do not try to tough it out or be the hero and neglect medical care. Make your medical care a priority before you even consider retaining an attorney, giving a statement or asserting a claim. It is critical that you get the timely medical attention you need and that you also follow your doctor's treatment recommendations. It is also vital that you consistently follow-up with your doctors and therapists to insure you are doing everything you can to help resolve your injuries. At VanMeveren Law Group, we know from our vast experience with bicycle accident cases that insurance companies and jurors are not sympathetic to folks who fail to get the treatment they need or simply ignore their doctor's orders.

Important Steps One Should Take After Being Involved In A Bicycle Accident

1. Obtain the name, address, license plate number and insurance information of the responsible party.

2. Contact emergency personnel and request that the police perform a full investigation and prepare an accident report.

3. Promptly seek medical attention if there is any question as to whether you've been injured.

4. If there are witnesses in the area, try to talk to those individuals, get their contact information and make certain that the investigating officers are aware of any witnesses.

5. If you are able and you have a cell phone or a camera, take photos of the scene, the involved vehicle, your bicycle and your injuries.

6. Keep a journal of the incident, your treatment and your limitations following the accident. As time passes and the memory of the incident fades, a clear recall of the events that caused the crash and the pain and inconveniences in the aftermath of the accident is important.

7. Don't discard your damaged bicycle or bicycle gear. You may be entitled to compensation for these items in addition to recovery for your bodily injuries. Your bicycle property may also be critical evidence in

determining the cause of the crash, proving fault and establishing damages.

8. Your health and well being should always be your top priority. But after you have been treated and released, do your research and find an experienced bicycle accident attorney. He or she should be skilled in the area of bicycle accident law and able to speak to you about preserving your rights and protecting your interests.

9. Remember that you are under no obligation to contact the other driver's insurance company, provide any statements (other than to the investigating officers) or sign any forms until you have consulted with an experienced attorney.

Importance Of Keeping A Log Or Journal Of Events Following A Bicycle Accident

We always advise our clients to keep a journal of their

daily activities from the date of the collision forward. This information is critical as the case develops because the injuries may involve head trauma or an extensive course of treatment over many months, sometimes years. Because our memories fade, it is *very* important to document the severity of the situation as well as the difficulties, the pain and the inconvenience associated with the recovery process. One should also document the inability to participate in activities that were once enjoyed. Our memories may be very sharp and clear in the days and weeks after the crash and we can certainly recall the details of the incident and the aftermath. But as time progresses, we forget how painful and upsetting the situation was in those first few weeks, what an inconvenience it was, how our work performance suffered, or how frustrating it was trying to care for our family.

Journaling post accident treatment, pain and inconveniences is vital in establishing a strong non-economic damages claim. Post accident claims and litigation procedures will undoubtedly include written or recorded statements, and in some cases, a deposition or trial testimony. These events may not take place for many months or even years after the incident. Thus, failure to document or journal your post accident experiences will make it difficult to accurately recall the severity of what you went through in those first few weeks and months following the crash. Referring to your journal in preparation for a deposition, a statement, or a hearing can refresh your memory and bring back into focus important issues that you may be unable to recall due to a head injury or with the passage of time.

Like any case, the primary issue that has to be addressed is the issue of fault or liability. Imagine being the victim of a bicycle accident. You were properly equipped and following the rules of the road when a truck turned left, directly into your path. The truck driver claims you rode through the 4-way stop without properly coming to a complete stop. Now you're injured, strapped with medical bills and missing time from work. You know you came to a complete stop, but the truck driver's insurance company is denying your damages claim.

Proof that the motorist caused the collision with the bicyclist is vital. Without sufficient evidence of fault, the the claim may be denied or the case could be dismissed. Colorado employs comparative fault when determining liability or fault in bicycle accident cases. In other words, a judge or jury can apportion any percentage of fault it deems appropriate to the responsible motorist or the injured bicyclist who is making the claim. Thus, if a judge or jury determine the bicyclist was inattentive, traveling too fast for conditions, or not riding in a reasonable manner, thereby causing or contributing to the crash, some or all of the fault could be allocated to the cyclist. During the pre-litigation claim process, the defendant's insurance adjuster, the claims representatives and defense attorneys are going to look for ways to demonstrate that the bicycle accident victim's own actions or inaction caused or contributed to his or her injuries. In Colorado, if the defendant's insurance company and defense counsel can prove that the bicyclist is at least *fifty percent* responsible, the result is a verdict in favor of the defendant motorist and there is no recovery for the injured cyclist. The overriding standard in any bicycle accident case is reasonable care. In other words, a cyclist is expected to operate a bike in a safe and careful manner at all times.

So it is vital that the issue of liability be closely examined before going forward with the case. Failure to secure solid evidence supporting a theory of liability could expose a bicyclist to a lawsuit that does not have any likelihood of resulting in a financial recovery. If that happens, the bicyclist could ultimately be responsible for his or her own costs in litigating the matter (filing fees, expert witness fees, etc.) *as well as* the opposing party's costs in defending the case.

Once the issue of liability is properly evaluated and it is determined that the motorist is at fault or more at fault than the bicyclist, then it is really a matter of comprehensively evaluating the nature and extent of the bicyclist's injuries. Thus, it is imperative that the injured cyclist seeks the appropriate medical care and has done everything he or she can to recover from the collision.

Post accident medical treatment is not only essential to one's well being, but is also critical to properly establishing damages in a bicycle accident case. This is not the time for an accident victim to be a hero, tough out injuries or ignore proper treatment protocol. A delay or failure to obtain the appropriate treatment for an extended period of time can create a situation where the other party's insurance company and their attorneys will have an argument that the injured bicyclist did *not* do everything possible to *mitigate* or to *reduce* the nature and extent of the injuries and damages. Gaps or delays in seeking medical care can also result in issues involving causation. In other words, lack of consistent treatment or a significant delay in treatment after the accident can raise doubts as to whether the injuries claimed are even related to the bicycle accident.

Laws Pertaining To Bicycle Riders In Colorado

Colorado law pertaining to bicyclists is set forth primarily in our Colorado Revised Statutes, under of Title 42. In a nutshell, bicyclist's duties and responsibilities are no different than the rights and responsibilities that pertain to motorists. For example, bicyclists using a roadway have to obey traffic lights and they have to obey stop signs. Unless preparing to make a left hand turn, overtaking a vehicle or avoiding road hazards, cyclists also have to ride with traffic on the right side of the road. If bicycling between sunset and sunrise, cyclists are required to use head lights, reflectors and tail lights.

Are There Laws Pertaining To Helmets, Lights and Safety Gear For Bicyclists In Colorado?

Surprisingly, bike helmets and safety gear such as mirrors and lights are not required while riding during daylight hours in Colorado. However, a red rear relflector is required, as well as lights and side reflectors while riding at night. Always check your local ordinances regarding bicycle equipment requirements. Notably, many states do require helmets, but Colorado does not have a specific helmet law for bicyclists or for motorcyclists. Nevertheless, statistics show that most fatalities involving bicyclists *are* associated with head injuries. Certainly, the best way to avoid being exposed to a very serious head injury and possibly death is to wear a helmet.

Again, if a claim involves a head injury and the bicyclist chose not to wear a helmet, the defendant may try to argue that that cyclist failed to *mitigate* the damages. The defense may try to claim the judge or jury should consider that an individual who failed to wear a helmet was not exercising *reasonable care.* In Colorado, if there is a head injury claim, but the cyclist chose not to wear a helmet, a judge or jury is *not* permitted to reduce or eliminate the cyclist's head injury damage claim. Thus, the fact that a cyclist was not wearing a helmet does not mean an insurance company can deny a cyclist's head injury claims.

Many cases, particularly those involving students who are on our Colorado State University campus, involve cyclists who choose not wear helmets. All of these cases, including claims where the damages involve head injuries to an unhelmeted rider, are viable claims. Despite Colorado law, the insurance company defending the claim and/or defense counsel may attempt to improperly use the cyclist's choice not to wear a helmet to their advantage to minimize or even eliminate the claim.

Is It Legal For A Motorist To Go Around A Bicycle?

Motorists have a duty to maintain a safe distance from a bicyclist at all times, including at least three feet when passing. When approached from behind by a motorist, most responsible bicyclists are going to move over to the right side of the roadway, onto the shoulder or into a bike lane when it is safe to do so. But there are situations where sections of the roads are not designed for safe bicycle travel on the far right side of the road and in those situations, the motorists need to exercise caution and maintain a safe distance from the bicyclist until it is reasonably safe to pass, while maintaining the *three feet* passing distance requirement.

Aggessive driving and driver impatience often create tragic outcomes for cyclists. Sadly, many motorists do not wait for a safe passing zones or a lawful passing area to overtake a cyclist and often try to pass at the worst posssible moment. The outcome of an unsafe passing maneuver is never good for the cyclist and usually results in vehicle contact with the cyclist, causing a crash and severe injuries. Bicyclists must protect themselves and should not be afraid to ride in the middle of the through lane of travel where it is unsafe to travel on the right side of the road. This maneuver by the cyclist could be life saving and is entirely legal in situations where hazards, road design or dangers on the right side of the roadway prevent safe travel on the right.

What Are The Most Common Driver Errors Contributing To Crashes With Cyclists?

Texting while driving has become one of the leading causes of car vs. car and car vs. bike crashes. Sadly, according to the *NHTSA*, more than 3,100 people were killed and 431,000 injured in distracted driving motor vehicle related accidents in 2014. Other common motorist errors arise from driver inattentiveness and impatience. Just the sight of a bicyclist can often cause frustration and anger when the motorist is in a hurry to get somewhere. Sadly, many drivers don't have the patience to slow down, even for just a moment, to accommodate a bicyclist. An aggressive passing maneuver in an unsafe passing area often leads to the vehicle sideswiping the cyclist, casuing the cyclist to lose control and crash. The outcome for the cyclist is never good under this scenario.

We also see a number of cases involving Colorado's *dooring law*. Again, the motorist's responsibility when they park on the side of a roadway is to ensure that the area surrounding the vehicle is safe and clear before they open their car door. This is a very common situation in which the motorist will simply pull over to the side of the road to park and inattentively open their car without considering that a bicyclist may be approaching from behind. When this occurs, the bicyclist strikes the open door, oftentimes resulting in very tragic outcomes and severe injuries.

What Is Comparative Fault In Bicycle Accident Claims?

Comparative fault essentially means that when a person's own actions contributed to his or her injuries, a judge or jury may reduce or eliminate any recovery by that percentage of fault apportioned to the injured party. Comparative fault laws vary from state to state. For example, in some states such as in Arizona, the claimant can be up to ninety-nine percent at fault and they can still recover one percent of their damages. In Colorado, consider the scales of justice as an example. If you think of the scales of justice, in order for the the injured bicyclist to prevail, he or she has to tip those scales, ever so slightly, in his or her favor. So in a case where a judge or jury determines that each party is 50% responsible, there will be no recovery for the injured cyclist. Thus, it is the claimant's responsibility and his or her attorney's responsibility to ensure that they present sufficient evidence to show that the responsible party is greater than fifty percent at fault in order to recover damages as a result of the defendant's negligent actions.

In comparative fault cases where the injured party is partially at fault, the full measure of damages can be limited or reduced. So if the recovery is, for example, $10,000 and a jury determines that the victim is forty percent responsible for his or her injuries, then that $10,000 verdict is reduced by $4,000. In other words, the recovery will be $6,000 in a case where the jury determines that the damages were $10,000, but there is 40% comparative fault on the part of the cyclist. Beware that insurance companies will use comparative fault issues to their advantage to minimize the claim. If they can locate any evidence indicating that the bicyclist was, for example, inattentive, wearing headphones, not wearing a helmet or failing to stop at a stop sign, they will try to use this evidence to their advantage in an attempt to reduce the claim or eliminate it in its entirety.

The issue of damages can also be impacted when there exists a lack of consistent medical treatment or a failure to treat properly following the crash. In these situations, the defense will certainly try to minimize the amount of recovery due to the injured party. Recovery limitations can also arise where the defense argues that claimant's damages are related to pre-existing injuries. In these situations, the defense will attempt to get a judge or jury to apportion some or all of the injuries or damages to an underlying condition or a prior injury as a way to minimize the claim and save the insurance company money.

What's The Difference Between A Bicycle Accident Case And Other Personal Injury Cases?

Most collisions on our roadways involve two motor vehicles, with the most common accidents being rear-end collisions. Rear-end car crashes most often involve two motor vehicles and generally result in minor injuries, usually soft tissue sprains and strains to the neck and back that typically resolve within a matter of weeks. In contrast, car vs. bike crashes almost always result in serious bodily injuries to the cyclist, including broken bones, road rash and head trauma. Just the nature of the size and weight disparity between a motor vehicle and a vulnerable cyclist is bound to result in much more serious injuries than being struck while traveling inside the protection of a car. Even in very minor car vs. bike accident cases, where the collision may occur at speeds as little as five to ten miles per hour, the damages to the cyclist can be severe and debilitating. Thus, due to the disparity between a motor vehicle and a virtually unprotected cyclist, even minor car vs. bike impacts can cause very serious injuries to the bicyclist.

What Is The Statute Of Limitations For A Bicycle Accident Claim?

In Colorado, the statute of limitations, or the period allowed for bringing a legal action, for car vs. bike crashes is three years. In fact, any case involving a bicycle accident that is associated with a motor vehicle, including anything with a motor, a motorcycle or a motor scooter, a car or a truck, falls under the three year statue of limitations. But beware of cases where there is a governmental entity involved. If the bicyclist is struck by a police officer or if the bicyclist encountered some danger or hazard on the road that was created by a governmental entity, then that period of time to assert the claim becomes much shorter. In Colorado, a claimant must notify or put on notice the governmental entity within one hundred and eighty-two (182) days and a failure to do so can result in an entire loss or dismissal of that claim. There are specific steps that must be taken when putting a governmental entity on notice. Thus, it is very important for the injured party to promptly determine who the potential defendants are going to be in the case, so as to protect oneself from missing the statutory notice period or the statute of limitations deadline. Always promptly consult an experienced bicycle accident attorney to determine the appropriate notice provisions, the statute of limitations and proper steps for moving forward with a claim.

Why Are Accident Reconstructionists And Re-Enactments Important In Bicycle Accident Cases?

Prompt bicycle accident investigation is critical. You can be assured that the insurance company for the at-fault driver is doing their own investigation. They often have an adjuster or an investigator working on the claim within minutes of the incident, looking for ways to minimize or defeat the claim by finding any evidence possible to deny liability. Once an injured cyclist retains VanMeveren Law Group, we promptly move forward with an investigation that includes obtaining a very detailed statement from our injured client, gathering all the facts and circumstances surrounding the incident. Next, we obtain the traffic accident report and contact all witnesses listed on the report. We also make contact with the investigating officer to confirm the facts surrounding the investigation. Where there is any question regarding fault or liability, we personally interview all investigating officers, the witnesses and promptly visit and photograph the scene of the incident.

We want to make certain that we are very familiar with the specific location where the crash occurred, always evaluating and looking for any evidence left on the roadway, such as skid marks, vehicle or bicycle debris. We also look for issues at the scene that may have caused or contributed to the crash, including obstructions to the involved parties' fields of vision, road damage and roadway design flaws. It is important to preserve all of the scene evidence, including the bicycle itself, for our accident reconstruction experts' evaluations and in preparation for trial.

There are many bicycle crash cases where there is a dispute with regard to who is at fault. Issues can include the speeds of the involved vehicles or bikes, the sequencing of the lights and the position of the car and bike on the roadway at impact. In these cases, we will engage specialized experts, including accident reconstructionists, traffic engineers and roadway design experts to closely examine the issues with regard to the vehicle dynamics, speeds, traffic light sequencing, perception/reaction times and the condition of the involved car and bike to help ensure that our liability claim is well-founded.

Do Most Bicycle Accident Claims Reach A Settlement Prior To Trial?

Most bike accident claims do reach a settlement before trial. A favorable settlement outcome is a direct result of our proactive approach to all cases. Due to our extensive experience with bicycle law, case evaluation and preparation, we are able to put our client's claims in a position where the insurance company knows we are thoroughly prepared to go to trial if a fair settlement offer is not promptly forthcoming. To put it another way, we organize a well-documented, essentially *bulletproof* claim that eliminates any issues regarding liability. Next, we thoroughly document in great detail the nature and extent of injuries, permanency, and damages. This diligent and thorough approach greatly improves the likelihood of producing a fair offer of settlement from the insurance company. In these situations, the insurance claims team knows that it is going to have to negotiate and settle the case in order to avoid the risk of greater exposure through a trial against a skilled and well prepared team of litigators at VanMeveren Law Group.

Settlement offers can vary widely, depending on who develops a bicycle accident claim. If an attorney fails to properly evaluate a case due to lack of experience or poor judgment, does not undertake a comprehensive investigation and analysis of all of the liability and damages issues, does not properly present the claim to the adjuster and/or fails to present all of the supporting evidence and documents associated with the claim, the result is usually an unreasonably low offer from the insurance company, or worse, none at all. These cases will often end up in an unnecessary trial because the insurance company is not going to take the unprepared attorney or the spotty claim seriously. Also, in the poorly developed cases, the attorney may not have the experience, resources or ability to effectively litigate the case. The insurance company will ferret out the attorney's weaknesses and the flaws in the case and use these factors to its advantage at trial, often at the expense of the innocent cyclist/victim. As a result, many cases end up in court, not because of the issues, but because the attorney failed to effectively develop and present the claim to the insurance carrier.

How Long Do Bicycle Accident Cases Take To Resolve?

The time necessary to resolve a bike accident case can vary from a few months to a few years. Colorado has a three year statute of limitations on car vs. bike cases. It is never advisable to rush into a settlement or trial. Our goal is that our client receives all of the treatment he or she needs before the case is fully evaluated and the claim submitted. We want to insure the client is comfortable moving forward only after treatment has ended and they have been discharged from care. The amount of time it takes to resolve a case is usually dictated by the severity of the injuries and the nature and extent of treatment. For example, if the claim involves a fractured wrist that is casted and it heals up in six weeks, we may be able to move forward and resolve that claim in as little as a few months. If the case involves traumatic brain injury, the case may not resolve for many years. Premature settlement of a high damages case is never advised because once the release is signed, the injured party can never re-open the claim. Diligent case preparation, keeping a close eye on the statute of limitations and constant follow up with our clients and their medical providers is vital to obtaining the best possible outcome and maximizing the recovery.

There is only one opportunity to settle with the responsible party and once the release agreement is signed, the right to assert any future claims is lost. So *never* rush or be pressured to reach a premature settlement where the full extent of the injuries and their permanency is unclear. Also, never resolve a case where the treating doctors have not provided a comprehensive discharge plan, including the permanency of the injuries and a prognosis of the future care needs. Prematurely moving forward and settling a case and then later learning that the lingering effects from the accident are necessitating more treatment can be disasterous, especially where the injured party does not have health insurance. You cannot go back to the defendant or insurance company a second time and seek an additional recovery.

The ultimate goal at VanMeveren Law Group is to help the client get all the necessary medical care they need and do everything we can to help the client reach a full recovery. Once a client has reached *maximum medical improvement*, we then move forward with preparation and submission of a comprehensive demand package to the insurance carrier, with the goal of obtaining the maximum available financial recovery in order to make our client whole again.

Is There Assistance Available To Clients In Paying For Medical Care During The Pendency Of Their Claim?

There are difficult cases where the prospective client comes into our office and does not have health insurance or any type of medical coverage. Fortunately, in Colorado, we can usually help the client obtain coverage, if eligibility requirements are met. There are instances where we've been able to get the medical coverage provider to *back date* the coverage so as to cover medical bills incurred as a result of the accident but before coverage was established.

If there is a criminal component to the claim, a victim's compensation fund and restitution may help with the client's accident related medical expenses and lost earnings. We will certainly help guide and support our clients through the criminal process and work diligently to obtain coverage through a variety of indigent care programs in Colorado, including Medicaid, if they qualify.

We also work closely with a number of medical providers in our community that will delay their claim for reimbursement for medical expenses until we are able to resolve or settle the injury claim. We can also assist the clients in working out reimbursement agreements with their providers so they can get the care that they need.

In many cases, the injured cyclist may also be eligible for medical payments coverage through his or her own auto insurer or the other driver's insurance carrier. Colorado law requires that every insurance carrier offer its insureds, at a minimum, $5,000 in medical payments coverage. Depending on the policy language and available coverage, there may be much higher limits in medical payments coverage the injured cyclist can use to cover medical costs.

SETTLE OR GO TO TRIAL?

Every one of our bike accident cases is analyzed on a weekly basis by our entire legal team. We maintain a very

detailed status report on each case and we keep our client involved in that process every step of the way. The most important thing we stress to our clients is to get all the medical care they need so they can reach *maximum medical improvement* as soon as possible. An injury claim is a huge disruption to one's life. We make sure that the client is supported in their medical care process and back to normal living as soon as medically and financially feasible. We want to insure that every client that retains us understands the process completely, is comfortable going forward with our recommendations and is advised of all settlement options. It is the client's case and ultimately his or her decision as to whether or not a settlement offer is accepted or a lawsuit is filed. Prior to engaging in any settlement discussions with the opposing party or insurance representatives, our case evaluation and comprehensive demand package will be reviewed with our client first and is always subject to his or her approval. Our goal going forward is to do everything we can to take the stress off our client and put the pressure on the insurance company to fairly and reasonably evaluate the severity of the claim and make an appropriate offer to settle the case.

We will do our own evaluations, based on our decades of personal injury case experience. We are able to make a comprehensive assessment, taking into consideration a settlement that would satisfy the client and take care of all of his or her injuries, damages and bills. The evaluation will also be consistent with what a jury would likely determine to be damages, in the event the case was litigated. We will review all pros and cons with the client before we take any steps toward litigation. If the insurance company is being unreasonable and they are not making a fair offer in the case and the settlement offer is below what is determined to be reasonable, appropriate and consistent with a jury verdict, our recommendation is going to be that we move aggressively in taking the next step of filing a lawsuit.

Our clients have a distinct advantage over folks that are trying to resolve matters on their own, working with inexperienced attorneys or working with an attorney who does not specialize in bicycle accident cases. At VanMeveren Law Group, we are able to *level the playing field* and let the insurance company know that we are well-prepared, serious and ready to litigate, if necessary. Thus, if we do not receive a fair offer, we are going to take matters to the next level and file suit. This puts additional pressure on the insurance company to make a fair offer, rather than risking greater exposure and expense to the company and its insured. We never take litigation lightly and any decision to litigate is thoroughly evaluated and reviewed with our client and always subject to his or her approval.

What Options Are Available To The Families Of The Deceased In Fatal Bicycle Accidents?

Bicyclist fatalities are becoming far too common and can wreak havoc on a family. In Colorado cases involving death, the responsible driver may face a variety of criminal charges as well as a civil wrongful death claim. If there is a pending criminal charge, we work closely with the district attorney to secure all evidence and to insure restitution is available, in the event the family incurs expenses as a result of the loss of a loved one.

Depending on the circumstances of the incident, a civil right of action may be available for families who lose a loved one. This would involve a wrongful death claim against the negligent motorist and in cases involving young drivers, the driver's parents. Civil wrongful death law is not designed to provide economic recovery for the decedent's medical bills or lost earnings. Rather, the qualifying family members have a right to assert damages and claims associated with their *emotional* losses, including the loss of love and support as well as the severe grief and emotional distress created by the tragedy.

Wrongful death claims can be only be asserted by certain family members. There is a specific Colorado statute that delineates which family members have a right of action. Wrongful death claims are not permissible in situations where a brother or sister is making a claim. If there is a loss of a child or spouse, the victims (spouse, children and possibly parents) may have claims. Consult with an experienced injury attorney to determine which specific family members have viable rights of action and in order to determine the statute of limitations.

What Types Of Damages Are Recoverable In A Bicycle Accident Claim?

Bicycle accident claims often involve a variety of damages, including but not limited to: damages for economic losses, non-economic claims for pain and suffering, disfigurement damages, and partial and permanent impairment claims.

Economic damages encompass past and future medical expenses, out-of-pocket costs and property losses, such as a damaged bicyle. Medical bills associated with the treatment received following a bike crash are also considered economic losses.

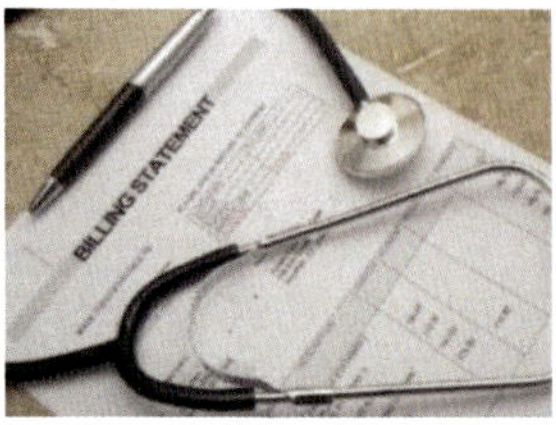

Economic damages also include past and future lost earnings. Because bicycle injury victims are often unable to work for extended periods of time during their injury recovery, this is an important damages component that must be thoroughly analyzed and documented, often with the assistance of an expert economist. Lost earnings claims should be well documented and supported with evidence including statements from the victim's employer's human resources department, tax returns, wage statements and W2s.

The bicycle accident victim is also entitled to out-of-pocket expenses. In many cases, there are items that are not covered by insurance or there are situations where the injured party may need to hire help to maintain their home. An injured cyclist may also need to buy medical equipment not covered by insurance to help in their recovery. Co-pays and deductibles that are not being covered by health insurance would also be considered compensable out-of-pocket losses.

In addition, any damage to the cyclist's personal property, including the damaged bicycle and gear involved in the accident, as well as the helmet, gloves, lights, glasses and bike computers, to name a few. A damaged cell phone or a broken laptop or other valuables in the cyclist's backpack are also considered recoverable property losses in a claim involving a bike accident.

Non-economic damages are also very important and include a number of sub-categories. Non-economic or non-pecuniary damages are not quantifiable in terms of dollars and cents. Rather, they are considered the *pain and suffering* component of damages. But non-economic damages include much more than just pain and suffering. Non- economic losses not only include the actual pain that the individual is suffering, but also the impact on the injured cyclist's quality of life, including how the accident has affected his or her ability to enjoy the activities that were enjoyed prior to the crash. These losses may include the physical and emotional impact on the ability to engage in hobbies as well as limitations on their ability to love and care for family. Non-economic losses may include things like an injured cyclist's inability to bend over to pick up a grandchild. Physical limitations following a bike crash are a very serious issue and can create a significant amount of emotional distress, not to mention the physical pain associated with trying trying to fight through the injury to be there for one's family.

Loss of consortium damages for the spouse of a victim are also compensable under the non-economic damages claim. If the evidence presented indicates that the spouse of an injured party has been affected and the relationship between the two has been negatively impacted or compromised, the spouse of a victim may also be entitled to compensation.

An additional category of damages includes the permanency of the injuries. The injured cyclist may have a permanent impairment where he or she is not able to fully return to their pre-accident activities. This could include a loss of strength, range of motion or permanent brain injury. Supporting medical evidence is vital to validate the extent and severity of permanent injury claims.

In addition, there may be damage associated with scarring or disfigurement. This can include road rash, deformities caused by fractured bones or surgical scars. Disfigurements can be a significant category of damages for anyone, but especially a young person who has to live with the scars for the rest of his or her life.

In special situations, punitive or exemplary damages may also apply to the claim. If our investigation reveals that the individual who caused the harm recklessly disobeyed legal responsibilities, such as driving under influence of alcohol or drugs, or engaging in some type of intentionally reckless conduct, a punitive damages claim may be warranted. In these instances, the amount of damages may be substantially enhanced, or in many cases doubled, if there is evidence indicating that the defendant engaged in reckless conduct. Punitive damages are a way of punishing the wrongdoer and are typically not covered by insurance.

What Does My Auto Insurance Have To Do With My Bicycle Accident Claim?

Before exposing yourself to the risks of road cycling, it is critical to make certain that you protect yourself and review all available insurance coverage. Many people are unaware just how important your own car insurance coverage can be if you are injured in an accident involving a car while riding your bike. There are multiple types of insurance coverage you'll want to have in place before you ride:

1. *Uninsured/Underinsured Motorists Coverage*: This type of insurance coverage can help cover your damages in the event that the person who hit you did not have insurance or did not have adequate insurance or assets to fully compensate you for your damages and losses.

2. *Medical Payments Coverage*: Med Pay coverage will cover reasonable and necessary medical expenses up to a set limit (usually $5,000.00), regardless of fault, in the event you are hit by a car while riding your bike.

3. *Health Insurance*: Make sure you have a good health insurance policy in place before you ride to pay for your medical expenses. The insurance company for the driver that hits you will not pay for any of your medical

care until the very end of your case so it's important to protect yourself and avoid exposure to medical bills during the pendency of your claim.

4. *Disability Insurance*: Due to the potential for severe and debilitating injuries following a bicycle accident, review your disability coverage to protect yourself in the event you are unable to return to work.

PRACTICE POINTERS:

1. Make sure you don't reject underinsured motorist or medical payments coverage when it's offered. DON'T OPT OUT!

2. Get the maximum med pay benefits available.

3. Talk to an experienced personal injury attorney about your insurance coverage.

What Factors Are Used By Insurance Companies To Dispute Claims?

Comparative Fault

The insurance adjuster is looking for any evidence that the bicyclist was being inattentive, traveling too fast, not appropriately stopping or failing to properly signal before the collision. A comparative fault argument will typically be raised if there is any evidence the cyclist caused or contributed to his or her own injuries. This is a common insurance adjuster tactic used to deny or minimize the value of the bicyclist’s claim. Again, jurors may consider all or none of that evidence in making their determination of fault. In those cases where the insurance company and its attorneys make arguments that the bicyclist was biking carelessly or being inattentive, the jury can consider that evidence as a way to reduce or eliminate the recovery for the bicyclist.

Failure To Follow Recommended Medical Treatment

Following the doctor’s orders and treatment recommendations is vital to a proper recovery following a bike crash. It's also an important factor in preserving all of the injured cyclist's damages and rights to a full recovery. This is another area where the insurance company will try to minimize the severity of the claim by arguing that, if in fact the bicyclist was truly injured, he or she would have treated more extensively and followed doctors' orders more closely. In many cases, the insurance adjuster or defense counsel will retain medical specialists who will review the medical records or examine the injured party and opine or testify that the injuries were minor, pre-existing, or the injured cyclist's failure to treat on a timely basis and follow the doctors' treatment guidelines contributed to the harm or delayed a full recovery. The defense of failure to *mitigate* damages is frequently raised by the insurance company as a means to poke holes in the the cyclist's injury claim. Common defenses also include claims that there were unreasonable delays or gaps in treatment, patient non-compliance, unnecessary/excessive treatment or unrelated care.

HERE'S WHAT YOU CAN EXPECT FROM YOUR VLG TEAM

The issue of liability needs to be comprehensively evaluated before any claim is submitted to the insurance company. Next, a thorough analysis of the injuries, treatment and medical history must be considered. Given the opportunity, the insurance carrier will attempt to shift much, if not all, of the liability or blame to the bicyclist. At VanMeveren Law Group, we will step into the shoes of the insurance company's adjuster and critically view the case from the other side's perspective. This approach is vital in order to proactively anticipate and mitigate the liability and damages issues raised by the defense. At VanMeveren Law Group, we are very familiar and well versed in the insurance company's tactics. We know what to expect and are prepared to respond in a manner that is most effective in bringing the claim to a prompt and successful resolution.

CAN I WORK WITH OTHER PARTY'S INSURANCE WITHOUT A LAWYER?

In situations where liability is clear, the injuries are minor, the course of treatment was short and the injured cyclist was able to make a full recovery without extensive medical care, case settlement without an attorney may be the best option. Under these circumstances, we do encourage direct contact with the at-fault driver's insurance company. But it's still important to gain a full understanding of your rights from an experienced attorney. Most attorney offices will offer a free, no obligation consultation to preliminarily assess the claim. But in some instances, engaging an attorney can delay the process and actually reduce the net recovery. In cases where the injuries are more serious or there is a dispute with respect to liability, do not talk to the insurance company, give a statement or sign any documents until after a comprehensive consultation with an experienced bicycle accident attorney.

Those individuals who do attempt to settle a serious injury claim *without* the aid of an experienced attorney do so at their peril. Unrepresented claimants are at a huge disadvantage when dealing with a seasoned claims adjuster. Remember, the adjuster's job is to deny, delay or minimize the value of the case. Insurance adjusters have a wealth of experience and settlement tools at their disposal which tend to confuse bike accident claimants and typically result in a settlement offer that is far below the true value of the claim. Once the claim is settled and the release signed, there's no second chance to reevaluate the case or reopen the claim if additional injuries or damages are later discoverd.

IMPORTANCE OF RETAINING A BICYCLE ACCIDENT ATTORNEY

The value in hiring experienced bicycle accident attorney is that they deal with these cases every day. Insurance carriers and their adjusters know who the attorneys are in the community that have experience with these types of cases. VanMeveren Law Group's attorneys include experienced bicyclists who have a unique familiarity with the issues that are encountered every day while riding on our Colorado roadways. An attorney with a solid foundation of actual bike riding experience and extensive experience in the handling of bicycle accident claims is vital to obtaining the best possible outcome.

Can I Afford An Experienced Bicycle Accident Attorney?

There is no cost to retain an experienced attorney. Do your research, get a referral from someone you trust and most importantly, find out what former clients are saying about this attorney. Research the *online reviews* and comments related to the firm you are considering retaining.

There are no upfront costs to you as the injured party, and do not be intimidated by the fact that you see a very well respected, busy attorney that you think you cannot afford. Most bicycle accident attorneys work on a percentage fee basis and are not going to require any advance payment on your case. The firm will only be paid if and when a recovery is obtained from the responsible party or their insured.

Can Any Respected Attorney Handle My Bike Accident Case?

Working with the right personal injury attorney, *especially in bike crash cases*, is crucial to obtaining the maximum available recovery. Not all attorneys are created equal. The unique liability issues in bike crash cases, the recovery process and multiple layers of insurance can all be very complicated. Taking an attorney recommendation from a friend and retaining an attorney who rarely handles bike accident cases, or is not familiar with bicycling on our Colorado roads, may hinder your ability to obtain a full and fair recovery.

Is A Bicycle Accident Claim A Relatively Easy Process?

Don't be naive when discussing your claim with the friendly insurance adjuster representing the responsible party. The adjuster's sole purpose is to save the insurance company money. The claimant is at a serious disadvantage not having experienced the process before. Unfamiliarity with the particular steps necessary to protect

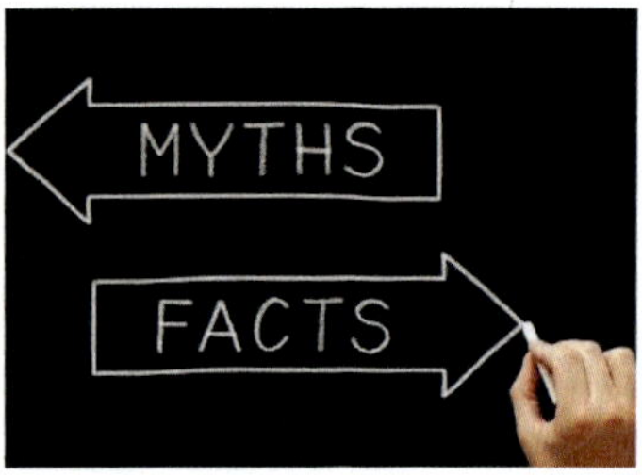

and preserve all components of the claim can seriously diminish the case value.

Understand that the insurance company will attempt to throw as many roadblocks as possible in your path in an effort to get you to give up on your claim. Despite all the clever, cute and friendly insurance company advertising, the insurance industry is a multi-billion dollar business that is purely profit-driven. It's all about economics and risk assessment for the big insurance companies with no concern for an injured party's well-being. The insurance company's roadblocks to the path of a fair recovery for a claimant are numerous and well designed to delay or deny payment for as long as possible.

VanMeveren Law Group's Experience In Handling Bicycle Accident Cases

Defending negligent motorists is where we developed a solid foundation in the evaluation and preparation of serious injury cases. For nearly 10 years, Mr. VanMeveren represented insurance companies and individuals in Colorado, Arizona and Wyoming, who seriously injured motorists, pedestrians and bicyclists. He transitioned his practice about fifteen years ago to work exclusively for bike accident victims and other victims of negligent actions. As an avid cyclist and triathlete for over twenty years, and a former insurance defense attorney, Mr. VanMeveren has the unique ability to comprehensively evaluate bicycle accident cases.

Uncommon Attributes Of VanMeveren Law Group

VanMeveren Law Group has an experienced team of attorneys who have all litigated serious injury cases. We have taken numerous cases to trial on behalf of injured victims and in defense of negligent motorists. Previously working for the insurance industry, we have handled very complex, serious injury cases and gained a specialized knowledge of how the big insurance companies evaluate and defend these claims. We now work exclusively as advocates for our injured clients. This strong foundation gives our firm the *inside track* as to how insurance adjusters, claims managers, and defense attorneys try to defend these cases.

Our distinct experience puts us in a position to move forward proactively and aggressively with our client's cases. We are continually putting extensive pressure on the insurance companies to do what is right: make a fair offer. Our collective legal experience, combined with a passion for bicycling, puts our client's cases in a strong position to obtain the best possible outcome.

What Are My Responsibilities As Bicycle Rider In Colorado?

The primary legal duties of Colorado cyclists are set forth in the following state statute:

C.R.S. 42-4-1412. Operation of bicycles and other human-powered vehicles.

1. Every person riding a bicycle or electrical assisted bicycle shall have all of the rights and duties applicable to the driver of any other vehicle under this article, except as to special regulations in this article and except as to those provisions which by their nature can have no application. Said riders shall comply with the rules set forth in this section and section 42-4-221, and, when using streets and highways within incorporated cities and towns, shall be subject to local ordinances regulating the operation of bicycles and electrical assisted bicycles as provided in section 42-4-111.

2. It is the intent of the general assembly that nothing contained in House Bill No. 1246, enacted at the second regular session of the fifty-sixth general assembly, shall in any way be construed to modify or increase the duty of the department of transportation or any political subdivision to sign or maintain highways or sidewalks or to affect or increase the liability of the state of Colorado or any political subdivision under the "Colorado Governmental Immunity Act", article 10 of title 24, C.R.S.

3. No bicycle or electrical assisted bicycle shall be used to carry more persons at one time than the number for which it is designed or equipped.

4. No person riding upon any bicycle or electrical assisted bicycle shall attach the same or himself or herself to any motor vehicle upon a roadway.

5. (a) Any person operating a bicycle or an electrical assisted bicycle upon a roadway at less than the normal speed of traffic shall ride in the right-hand lane, subject to the following conditions:

(I) If the right-hand lane then available for traffic is wide enough to be safely shared with overtaking vehicles, a bicyclist shall ride far enough to the right as judged safe by the bicyclist to facilitate the movement of such overtaking vehicles unless other conditions make it unsafe to do so.

(II) A bicyclist may use a lane other than the right-hand lane when:

(A) Preparing for a left turn at an intersection or into a private roadway or driveway;

(B) Overtaking a slower vehicle; or

(C) Taking reasonably necessary precautions to avoid hazards or road conditions.

(III) Upon approaching an intersection where right turns are permitted and there is a dedicated right-turn lane, a bicyclist may ride on the left-hand portion of the dedicated right-turn lane even if the bicyclist does not intend to turn right.

(b) A bicyclist shall not be expected or required to:

(I) Ride over or through hazards at the edge of a roadway, including but not limited to fixed or moving objects, parked or moving vehicles, bicycles, pedestrians, animals, surface hazards, or narrow lanes; or

(II) Ride without a reasonable safety margin on the right-hand side of the roadway.

(c) A person operating a bicycle or an electrical assisted bicycle upon a one-way roadway with two or more marked traffic lanes may ride as near to the left-hand curb or edge of such roadway as judged safe by the bicyclist, subject to the following conditions:

(I) If the left-hand lane then available for traffic is wide enough to be safely shared with overtaking vehicles, a bicyclist shall ride far enough to the left as judged safe by the bicyclist to facilitate the movement of such overtaking vehicles unless other conditions make it unsafe to do so.

(II) A bicyclist shall not be expected or required to:

(A) Ride over or through hazards at the edge of a roadway, including but not limited to fixed or moving objects, parked or moving vehicles, bicycles, pedestrians, animals, surface hazards, or narrow lanes; or

(B) Ride without a reasonable safety margin on the left-hand side of the roadway.

6. (a) Persons riding bicycles or electrical assisted bicycles upon a roadway shall not ride more than two abreast except on paths or parts of roadways set aside for the exclusive use of bicycles.

(b) Persons riding bicycles or electrical assisted bicycles two abreast shall not impede the normal and reasonable movement of traffic and, on a laned roadway, shall ride within a single lane.

7. A person operating a bicycle or electrical assisted bicycle shall keep at least one hand on the handlebars at all times.

8. (a) A person riding a bicycle or electrical assisted bicycle intending to turn left shall follow a course described in sections 42-4-901 (1), 42-4-903, and 42-4-1007 or may make a left turn in the manner prescribed in paragraph (b) of this subsection (8).

   (b) A person riding a bicycle or electrical assisted bicycle intending to turn left shall approach the turn as closely as practicable to the right-hand curb or edge of the roadway. After proceeding across the intersecting roadway to the far corner of the curb or intersection of the roadway edges, the bicyclist shall stop, as much as practicable, out of the way of traffic. After stopping, the bicyclist shall yield to any traffic proceeding in either direction along the roadway that the bicyclist had been using. After yielding and complying with any official traffic control device or police officer regulating traffic on the highway along which the bicyclist intends to proceed, the bicyclist may proceed in the new direction.

   (c) Notwithstanding the provisions of paragraphs (a) and (b) of this subsection (8), the transportation commission and local authorities in their respective jurisdictions may cause official traffic control devices to be placed on roadways and thereby require and direct that a specific course be traveled.

9. (a) Except as otherwise provided in this subsection (9), every person riding a bicycle or electrical assisted bicycle shall signal the intention to turn or stop in accordance with

section 42-4-903; except that a person riding a bicycle or electrical assisted bicycle may signal a right turn with the right arm extended horizontally.

(b) A signal of intention to turn right or left when required shall be given continuously during not less than the last one hundred feet traveled by the bicycle or electrical assisted bicycle before turning and shall be given while the bicycle or electrical assisted bicycle is stopped waiting to turn. A signal by hand and arm need not be given continuously if the hand is needed in the control or operation of the bicycle or electrical assisted bicycle.

10. (a) A person riding a bicycle or electrical assisted bicycle upon and along a sidewalk or pathway or across a roadway upon and along a crosswalk shall yield the right-of-way to any pedestrian and shall give an audible signal before overtaking and passing such pedestrian. A person riding a bicycle in a crosswalk shall do so in a manner that is safe for pedestrians.

(b) A person shall not ride a bicycle or electrical assisted bicycle upon and along a sidewalk or pathway or across a roadway upon and along a crosswalk where such use of bicycles or electrical assisted bicycles is prohibited by official traffic control devices or local ordinances. A person riding a bicycle or electrical assisted bicycle shall dismount before entering any crosswalk where required by official traffic control devices or local ordinances.

(c) A person riding or walking a bicycle or electrical assisted bicycle upon and along a sidewalk or pathway or across a roadway upon and along a crosswalk shall have all the rights and duties applicable to a pedestrian under the same circumstances, including, but not limited to, the rights and duties granted and required by section 42-4-802.

(d) (Deleted by amendment, L. 2005, p. 1353, § 1, effective July 1, 2005.)

11. (a) A person may park a bicycle or electrical assisted bicycle on a sidewalk unless prohibited or restricted by an official traffic control device or local ordinance.

(b) A bicycle or electrical assisted bicycle parked on a sidewalk shall not impede the normal and reasonable movement of pedestrian or other traffic.

(c) A bicycle or electrical assisted bicycle may be parked on the road at any angle to the curb or edge of the road at any location where parking is allowed.

(d) A bicycle or electrical assisted bicycle may be parked on the road abreast of another such bicycle or bicycles near the side of the road or any location where parking is allowed in such a manner as does not impede the normal and reasonable movement of traffic.

(e) In all other respects, bicycles or electrical assisted bicycles parked anywhere on a highway shall conform to the provisions of part 12 of this article regulating the parking of vehicles.

12. (a) Any person who violates any provision of this section commits a class 2 misdemeanor traffic offense; except that section 42-2-127 shall not apply.

(b) Any person riding a bicycle or electrical assisted bicycle who violates any provision of this article other than this section which is applicable to such a vehicle and for which a penalty is specified shall be subject to the same specified penalty as any other vehicle; except that section 42-2-127 shall not apply.

13. Upon request, the law enforcement agency having jurisdiction shall complete a report concerning an injury or death incident that involves a bicycle or electrical assisted bicycle on the roadways of the state, even if such accident does not involve a motor vehicle.

14. Except as authorized by section 42-4-111, the rider of an electrical assisted bicycle shall not use the electrical motor on a bike or pedestrian path.

DISCLAIMER

This publication is intended to be informational only. No legal advice is being given, and no attorney-client relationship is intended to be created by reading this material. If you are facing legal issues, whether criminal or civil, seek professional legal counsel to get your questions answered.

VANMEVEREN LAW GROUP, P.C.
2038 Caribou Drive, Suite 101
Fort Collins, CO 80525
(970) 495-9741
www.vanmeverenlaw.com

Made in the USA
Coppell, TX
11 November 2026

11803121R00048

Cut By: Johanna J **Qty** 47 **Date** 11.8.26

Scanned By: ____ **Qty** ____ **Date** ____

Scanned Batch ID's

____ ____ ____

Notes / Exceptions

____